Practical Pre-School

Planning for Learning through Opposites

REVISED EDITION

by Judith Harries   Illustrated by Cathy Hughes

Contents

2-3 Making plans

4-7 Using the Early Learning Goals

8-9 Week 1: Happy and sad

10-11 Week 2: Big and small

12-13 Week 3: Old and new

14-15 Week 4: Hot and cold

16-17 Week 5: Loud and quiet

18-19 Week 6: Up and down

20 Bringing it all together - Pyjama party

21 Resources

22 Collecting evidence of children's learning

23 Skills overview of six-week plan

24 Home links

Inside back cover Parent's Page

Published by Step Forward Publishing Limited
St Jude's Church, Dulwich Road, Herne Hill, London, SE24 0PB Tel. 020 7738 5454
Revised edition © Step Forward Publishing Limited 2008
First edition © Step Forward Publishing Limited 2003
www.practicalpreschool.com
All rights reserved. No part of this publication may be reproduced, stored in a retrieval system, or transmitted by any means, electronic, mechanical, photocopied or otherwise, without the prior permission of the publisher.
Planning for Learning through Opposites ISBN: 978 1 90457 569 6

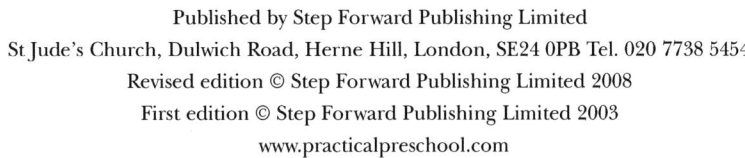

Making plans

Why plan?

The purpose of planning is to make sure that all children enjoy a broad and balanced curriculum. All planning should be useful. Plans are working documents that you spend time preparing, but which should later repay your efforts. Try to be concise. This will help you in finding information quickly when you need it.

Long-term plans

Preparing a long-term plan, which maps out the curriculum during a year or even two, will help you to ensure that you are providing a variety of activities and are meeting the statutory requirements of the *Statutory Fraework for the Early Years Foundation Stage: Setting the Standards for Learning, Development and Care for Children from Birth to Five* (2007).

Your long-term plan need not be detailed. Divide the time period over which you are planning into fairly equal sections, such as half terms. Choose a topic for each section. Young children benefit from making links between the new ideas they encounter so as you select each topic, think about the time of year in which you plan to do it. A topic about minibeasts will not be very successful in November!

Although each topic will address all the learning areas, some could focus on a specific area. For example, a topic on 'Opposites' would lend itself well to activities relating to Problem Solving, Reasoning and Numeracy and Physical Development. Another topic might particularly encourage the appreciation of stories. Try to make sure that you provide a variety of topics in your long-term plans.

Autumn 1	All about me
Autumn 2	Toys/Christmas
Spring 1	Opposites
Spring 2	Growth
Summer 1	Sounds
Summer 2	Water

Medium-term plans

Medium-term plans will outline the contents of a topic in a little more detail. One way to start this process is by brainstorming on a large piece of paper. Work with your team writing down all the activities you can think of which are relevant to the topic. As you do this it may become clear that some activities go well together. Think about dividing them into themes. The topic of 'Opposites', for example, has themes such as 'Happy and sad', 'Big and small', 'Old and new' and 'Up and down'. At this stage it is helpful to make a chart. Write the theme ideas down the side of the chart and put a different area of learning at the top of each column. Now you can insert your brainstormed ideas and will quickly see where there are gaps. As you complete the chart take account of children's earlier experiences and provide opportunities for them to progress.

Refer back to the *Early Years Foundation Stage* document and check that you have addressed as many different aspects of it as you can. Once all your medium-term plans are complete make sure that there are no neglected areas.

Day-to-day plans

The plans you make for each day will outline aspects such as:

- resources needed;
- the way in which you might introduce activities;

Making plans

- the organisation of adult help;
- size of the group;
- timing;
- key vocabulary.

Identify the learning and the ELGs that each activity is intended to promote. Make a note of any assessments or observations that you are likely to carry out. On your plans make notes of activities that were particularly successful, or any changes you would make another time.

A final note

Planning should be seen as flexible. Not all groups meet every day, and not all children attend every day. Any part of the plan can be used independently, stretched over a longer period or condensed to meet the needs of any group. You will almost certainly adapt the activities as children respond to them in different ways and bring their own ideas, interests and enthusiasms. The important thing is to ensure that the children are provided with a varied and enjoyable curriculum that meets their individual developing needs.

Using the book

- Collect or prepare suggested resources as listed on page 21.
- Read the section which outlines links to the Early Learning Goals (pages 4-7) and explains the rationale for the topic of 'Opposites'.
- For each weekly theme two activities are described in detail as an example to help you in your planning and preparation. Key vocabulary, questions and learning opportunities are identified.
- The topic of 'Opposites' has a particular emphasis on a different area of learning each week. This will be highlighted and one of the above activities will relate to this area.
- The skills chart on page 23 will help you to see at a glance which aspects of children's development are being addressed as a focus each week.
- As children take part in the 'Opposites' topic activities, their learning will progress. Collecting evidence on page 22 explains how you might monitor children's achievements.
- Find out on page 20 how the topic can be brought together in a grand finale involving parents, children and friends.
- There is additional material to support the working partnership of families and children in the form of a 'Home links' page, and a photocopiable parent's page at the back of the book.

It is important to appreciate that the ideas presented in this book will only be a part of your planning. Many activities that will be taking place as routine in your group may not be mentioned. For example, it is assumed that sand, dough, water, puzzles, floor toys and large scale apparatus are part of the ongoing pre-school experience, as are the opportunities which increasing numbers of groups are able to offer for children to develop ICT skills. Role-play areas, stories, rhymes and singing, and group discussion times are similarly assumed to be happening each week, although they may not be a focus for described activities.

Using the 'Early Learning Goals'

Having chosen your topic and made your medium-term plans you can use the *Statutory Framework for the Early Years Foundation Stage* to highlight the key learning opportunities your activities will address. The Early Learning Goals are split into six areas: Personal, Social and Emotional Development; Communication, Language and Literacy; Problem Solving, Reasoning and Numeracy; Knowledge and Understanding of the World; Physical Development and Creative Development. Do not expect each of your topics to cover every goal but your long-term plans should allow for all of them to be addressed by the time a child enters Year 1.

The following sections highlight parts of the Statutory Framework in point form to show what children are expected to be able to do in each area of learning by the time they enter Year 1. These points will be used throughout this book to show how activities for a topic on 'Opposites' link to these expectations. For example, Personal, Social and Emotional Development point 7 is 'form good relationships with adults and peers'. Activities suggested which provide the opportunity for children to do this will have the reference PS7. This will enable you to see which parts of the Early Learning Goals are covered in a given week and plan for areas to be revisited and developed.

In addition, you can ensure that activities offer variety in the goals to be encountered. Often a similar activity may be carried out to achieve different learning objectives. For example, during this topic the children will design and make pop-up puppets. They will be developing aspects of Knowledge and Understanding of the World as they select resources and tools to assemble the puppets. They will also be gaining experience of Creative Development as they paint and decorate the puppets and Communication, Language and Literacy as they use them to invent dialogues and stories.

Personal, Social and Emotional Development (PS)

This area of learning covers important aspects of development that affect the way children learn, behave and relate to others.

By the end of the Early Years Foundation Stage, children will:

PS1   Continue to be interested, excited and motivated to learn.
PS2   Be confident to try new activities, initiate ideas and speak in a familiar group.
PS3   Maintain attention, concentrate, and sit quietly when appropriate.
PS4   Respond to significant experiences, showing a range of feelings when appropriate.
PS5   Have a developing awareness of their own needs, views and feelings, and be sensitive to the needs, views and feelings of others.
PS6   Have a developing respect for their own cultures and beliefs and those of other people.
PS7   Form good relationships with peers and adults.
PS8   Work as part of a group or class taking turns and sharing fairly; understanding that there need to be agreed values and codes of behaviour for groups of people, including adults and children, to work harmoniously.
PS9   Understand what is right, what is wrong and why.
PS10 Consider the consequences of their words and actions for themselves and others.
PS11 Dress and undress independently and manage their own personal hygiene.
PS12 Select and use activities and resources independently.
PS13 Understand that people have different needs, views, cultures and beliefs that need to be treated with respect.

PS14 Understand that they can expect others to treat their needs, views, cultures and beliefs with respect.

The topic of 'Opposites' provides valuable opportunities for children to develop awareness of their own needs and feelings and be sensitive to the needs and feelings of others. Time spent discussing feelings, losing things and scary sounds will encourage children to speak in a group, to share their feelings and to consider consequences. By playing circle games and 'Snakes and ladders' children will learn to take turns and to listen to each other. Many of the areas outlined above will also be covered as children carry out the activities in other learning areas. For example, when children play physical games and join in songs and number rhymes they will also be developing PS8.

Communication, Language and Literacy (L)

By the end of the EYFS, children should:

L1 Interact with others, negotiating plans and activities and taking turns in conversation.
L2 Enjoy listening to and using spoken and written language, and readily turn to it in their play and learning.
L3 Sustain attentive listening, responding to what they have heard with relevant comments, questions or actions.
L4 Listen with enjoyment and respond to stories, songs and other music, rhymes and poems and make up their own stories, songs, rhymes and poems.
L5 Extend their vocabulary, exploring the meanings and sounds of new words.
L6 Speak clearly and audibly with confidence and control and show awareness of the listener.
L7 Use language to imagine and recreate roles and experiences.
L8 Use talk to organise, sequence and clarify thinking, ideas, feelings and events.
L9 Hear and say sounds in words in the order in which they occur.
L10 Link sounds to letters, naming and sounding the letters of the alphabet.
L11 Use their phonic knowledge to write simple regular words and make phonetically plausible attempts at more complex words.
L12 Explore and experiment with sounds, words and texts.
L13 Retell narratives in the correct sequence, drawing on language patterns of stories.
L14 Read a range of familiar and common words and simple sentences independently.
L15 Know that print carries meaning and, in English, is read from left to right and top to bottom.
L16 Show an understanding of the elements of stories, such as main character, sequence of events and openings and how information can be found in non-fiction texts to answer questions about where, who, why and how.
L17 Attempt writing for various purposes, using features of different forms such as lists, stories and instructions.
L18 Write their own names and other things such as labels and captions, and begin to form simple sentences, sometimes using punctuation.
L19 Use a pencil and hold it effectively to form recognisable letters, most of which are correctly formed.

Several opportunities are given for children to respond to well-known picture books and stories, retelling and writing stories, adding sound effects, using drama, and reinforcing and extending their vocabulary. Making invitations for grandparent's day, new baby cards and name strings will help children to develop their

early writing skills. Throughout the topic, children are encouraged to explore the sounds of words and rhymes, and to see some of their ideas recorded in poems, pictures, words and on tape. Role-play areas are described that will allow children to use their imaginations as they play in the bear cave and enjoy the hot/cold areas.

Problem Solving, Reasoning and Numeracy (N)

By the end of the EYFS, children should:

N1 Say and use number names in order in familiar contexts.
N2 Count reliably up to ten everyday objects.
N3 Recognise numerals 1 to 9.
N4 use developing mathematical ideas and methods to solve practical problems.
N5 In practical activities and discussion, begin to use the vocabulary involved in adding and subtracting.
N6 Use language such as 'more' or 'less' to compare two numbers.
N7 Find one more or one less than a number from one to ten.
N8 Begin to relate addition to combining two groups of objects and subtraction to 'taking away'.
N9 Use language such as 'greater', 'smaller', 'heavier' or 'lighter' to compare quantities.
N10 Talk about, recognise and recreate simple patterns.
N11 Use language such as 'circle' or 'bigger' to describe the shape and size of solids and flat shapes.
N12 Use everyday words to describe position

The theme of 'Opposites' provides a meaningful context for mathematical activities. Matching, sorting and counting skills are used to play games with sound sources, instruments and dice. There are several fun activities exploring pattern including threading beads and using simple written symbols. Measuring activities use hand spans to measure different items and boxes to estimate weight. Children use problem solving skills to create a birthday chart to show children's ages. There are plenty of opportunities for children to use mathematical language during water and sand play and positional language as they make a fairground number frieze.

Knowledge and Understanding of the World (K)

By the end of the EYFS, children should:

K1   Investigate objects and materials by using all of their senses as appropriate.
K2   Find out about, and identify, some features of living things, objects and events they observe.
K3   Look closely at similarities, differences, patterns and change.
K4   Ask questions about why things happen and how things work.
K5   Build and construct with a wide range of objects, selecting appropriate resources and adapting their work where necessary.
K6   Select the tools and techniques they need to shape, assemble and join materials they are using.
K7   Find out about and identify the uses of everyday technology and use information and communication technology and programmable toys to support their learning.
K8   Find out about past and present events in their own lives, and in those of their families and other people they know observe.
K9   Find out about and identify features in the place they live and the natural world.
K10 Find out about their environment, and talk about those features they like and dislike.
K11 Begin to know about their own cultures and beliefs and those of other people.

As children carry out the activities in this topic, they will discover many opportunities to use all their senses to make observations and find out about their environment. They can investigate ice, the volume of sound, and floating and sinking. Making a family tree will enable children to find out about their own past. There are opportunities to use tools and technology as they use magnifying glasses and cameras to take photographs of each other. There are several activities that focus on designing and constructing models including puppets, vehicles, boats and shakers. As they enjoy making jelly and ice cubes, they will look closely at similarities, differences and change. Throughout all the activities children should be given the chance to talk about their experiences and ask questions.

Physical Development (PD)

By the end of the EYFS, children should:

PD1 Move with confidence, imagination and in safety.
PD2 Move with control and coordination.
PD3 Travel around, under, over and through balancing and climbing equipment.
PD4 Show awareness of space, of themselves and of others.
PD5 Recognise the importance of keeping healthy and those things which contribute to this.
PD6 Recognise the changes that happen to their bodies when they are active.
PD7 Use a range of small and large equipment
PD8 Handle tools, objects, construction and malleable materials safely and with increasing control.

Activities such as making mobiles, packing boxes, measuring snakes and handling playdough will offer experience of PD8. As children use bean bags, hoops, balls, and climbing apparatus they will use a range of equipment. Moving to music and along straight and wiggly lines will develop control and coordination. As children join in the warm-up session they will become aware of how their bodies change when active. Several collaborative games offer opportunities to move with confidence, imagination and awareness of space.

Creative Development (C)

By the end of the EYFS, children should:

C1 Respond in a variety of ways to what they see, hear, smell, touch and feel.
C2 Express and communicate their ideas, thoughts and feelings by using a widening range of materials, suitable tools, imaginative and role-play, movement, designing and making, and a variety of songs and musical instruments.
C3 Explore colour, texture, shape, form and space in two or three dimensions.
C4 Recognise and explore how sounds can be changed, sing simple songs from memory, recognise repeated sounds and sound patterns and match movements to music.
C5 Use their imagination in art and design, music, dance, imaginative and role play and stories.

During this topic, children will experience working with a variety of materials as they design and make masks, hot/cold collages and weaving trays, and dress life-size figures. They will be able to develop painting skills as they make self-portraits, paint with ice cubes, experiment with big/small paintings and press printing. C4 is explored as the children sing songs and explore musical opposites. They can use their imagination in drama activities such as happy/sad masks, and acting out various nursery rhymes. Throughout all the activities children are encouraged to talk about what they see and feel as they communicate their ideas in painting, collage, music, mime and drama.

Week 1
Happy and sad

Personal, Social and Emotional Development
- Introduce the theme by talking about the word 'opposite'. Play a circle game (see activity below). (PS1, 3, 8)
- During circle time, encourage children to pull happy and sad faces. Pass round a mirror so they can look at their expressions. Ask children what makes them feel happy or sad. Pass a smile around the circle. (PS1, 4, 5)
- Play 'mirrors'. Ask children to sit facing a partner and copy them. Try 'mirror opposites' – if your partner smiles, you must look sad. (PS3, 5)
- Read Dogger by Shirley Hughes (Red Fox). How do the children feel when they lose a special toy? (PS3, 5, 9)

Communication, Language and Literacy
- Make a class book of opposites beginning with 'happy and sad' and add to it throughout the topic. Ask children to draw or cut out pictures of happy and sad faces. Make up stories about why the faces look happy or sad. (L4, 7, 17)
- Make a collection of opposite books and puzzles. Compile a list of opposite words and display on pre-cut star shapes around the room. (L4, 5)
- Ask the children if they can tell you any funny jokes or stories. Write them into a book to help make people smile. (L2, 4, 6)

Problem Solving, Reasoning and Numeracy
- Use pre-cut sticky paper shapes to make happy and sad faces. Ask children to name the shapes they have chosen. (N1)
- Enjoy using this food rhyme:
  Five fish fingers for your tea.
  Will you share just one with me?
  Eating one will make me glad.
  There's four left, please don't be sad.
  Four fish fingers…(N1, 5, 7,8)

Knowledge and Understanding of the World
- Help children to take photographs of each other looking happy/sad. (K7)
- Make happy/sad pop-up puppets. Use wooden spoons and help children to paint a happy face on one side and a sad one on the other. Decorate short cardboard tubes and make the spoons pop up. (K5, 6)

Physical Development
- Play 'throw that feeling'. Sit in a circle and throw a beanbag to a child. Ask them to show you a feeling with their face. Throw the beanbag to another child, and so on. (PD7)
- Make happy/sad mobiles from salt dough (see activity opposite). (PD8)
- Play 'happy and sad'. Ask the children to dance around with smiley faces when they hear the music. When it stops they must stand still and look sad. (PD1, 2, 4)

Creative Development
- Sing the 'Opposites' song from Bingo Lingo (see Resources).
- Sing 'If you're happy and you know it, clap your hands'. Sing it slowly and change to 'If you're sad and you know it, look like this' and pull sad faces. (C4)
- Ask children to paint happy/sad self-portraits. Use hand mirrors. Scribe why the faces are happy or sad. (C3)
- Use paper plates to make happy/sad masks. Use in a drama situation. Choose other opposite feelings such as brave/scared, asleep/awake or angry/calm. (C2)

Activity: Can you find the opposite?

Learning opportunity: Playing a collaborative game to introduce opposites.

Early Learning Goal: Personal, Social and Emotional Development. Children will work as part of a group, taking turns and sharing fairly.

Resources: A selection of books on the topic of opposites (see the resources section); a selection of pairs of opposites such as old/new shoes, big/small balls, empty/full bottles, tall/short candles, black/white boxes,

happy/sad faces, heavy/light bags; a bean bag.
Organisation: Whole group.

Key vocabulary: Opposite words, pairs.

What to do: Sit in a circle with the opposite pairs mixed up in the middle. Show the children the big ball and ask if anyone can show you the small ball. Look at the big and small balls together and explain that they are 'opposite' to each other. Can the children show you any other opposites?

Read any book about opposites. Teach the children this simple song:

Can you find the opposite, opposite, opposite?
Can you find the opposite of _____?
(Tune: 'London Bridge')

Choose one item from the centre of the circle, such as the old shoe. Ask them if it is old or new? Pass the beanbag around the circle as you sing the song. Whoever is holding it when the song ends must find the 'new' shoe to make a pair. Give each child a turn.

The final song:
We have found the opposites, opposites, opposites.
We have found the opposites, and now it's time to stop!

Activity: Happy/sad mobiles

Learning opportunity: Working imaginatively with a malleable material.

Early Learning Goal: Physical Development. Children will be able to handle tools, objects and malleable materials safely and with increasing control.

Resources: A quantity of salt dough made using 2 cups of plain flour, 1 cup of water, 1 cup of salt, 1 tbsp oil; rolling pins; different-sized round cutters; brushes; paint; straws; string or ribbon; plastic hoop or metal coat hanger.

Organisation: Small group.

Key vocabulary: Circle, cutter, face, happy, smile, sad, tears.

What to do: Work with a small group of children to measure and mix the salt dough. Explain that it is not edible! Give children time to experiment with the dough. Show them how to roll it out, not too thin, and cut out different-sized circles. Help them to make a small hole near the edge of each circle using a straw.
Talk about happy and sad faces. These can be painted later or made by punching out small circles for eyes and adding mouths made from thin sausages of dough in a happy or sad shape. Use a damp brush to join pieces of dough together.

Bake the dough very slowly in a cool oven, preferably overnight. The children can paint the faces on both sides. Help them to thread various lengths of ribbon through the holes and hang faces from the hoop. Display where visitors can see them.

Display

Paint two giant faces, one with a happy smile and the other looking sad, and display them on the wall. Mount the children's happy/sad photographs and self-portraits underneath.

Make a puppet theatre from a big cardboard box. Use drapes to make curtains. Place on a table and encourage children to perform puppet shows using the pop-up

Week 2
Big and small

Personal, Social and Emotional Development
- Read Where's my Teddy? by Jez Alborough (Walker). Talk about how big things look to small children. (PS2, 4, 5)
- Bring in a big bear and a small bear with a collection of different-sized clothes for the children to dress them. Look at baby clothes and clothes that are too big. Ask children to try clothes on for fun. Talk about fit. (PS2, 5, 11)
- Go on an opposites hunt looking for big and small things. Make a list of how many other opposites you spot. Don't forget to listen as well as look! (PS1, 8)

Communication, Language and Literacy
- Read Can't You Sleep, Little Bear? by Martin Waddell (Walker). Create a role-play area of the bear cave (see activity opposite). (L1, 4, 7)
- Make a collection of size opposites such as long/short, fat/thin, narrow/wide and heavy/light. Scribe them on suitably shaped cards. (L5, 12)
- Point out differences between some big (capital) and small letters. Help children to write their names on pre-cut circles using a capital letter at the beginning. Join letters into a name string. (L10, 18)

Problem Solving, Reasoning and Numeracy
- Use threading beads to make a big, small, big, small pattern. Ask children to make up their own repeating patterns. (N10, 11)
- Use different-sized hands as non-standard measures (see activity opposite). (N3, 6, 11)
- Fill same-sized boxes with different materials. Help children to estimate weight and put them in order (lightest to heaviest). Check results using scales. (N4, 9)
- Explore the opposites 'empty' and 'full' using different-sized containers in the water and sand trays. How many small cups does it take to fill a bottle? Ask them to half-fill a bucket. Is it half full or half empty? (N4)

Knowledge and Understanding of the World
- Invite children to use magnifying glasses to observe small things around the nursery, inside and outside. Talk about how they make thinks look bigger. (K1, 2)
- Use different-sized construction toys to make big and small model vehicles. (K5)
- Work as a group to make a house, vehicle or rocket out of a big cardboard box. Use small match boxes or film canisters to make keepsake or treasure boxes. (K5, 6)

Physical Development
- Ask children to move around the room taking big steps in time to a steady beat on the drum. Try little running steps in time to a faster beat. (PD2, 4)
- Use playdough or clay to make long and short snakes. Measure the longest and the shortest. (PD8)
- Play with big hoops and small quoits, big and small balls. (PD7)

Creative Development
- Work in groups to paint big pictures. Use big brushes, big pots of paint and a huge canvas. Contrast this with using tiny pieces of paper, small brushes and paint trays. (C3)
- Enjoy acting out the story, singing and adding

Planning for Learning through Opposites

10   Practical Pre-School

instruments to 'The Enormous Turnip' from Three Singing Pigs (see Resources). (C2)
- Ask children to imagine being really small like a minibeast. What would the world look like? Act out 'A day in the life of a ladybird/ant'. (C5)

Activity: Big bear, little bear

Learning opportunity: Using the role-play area to develop imaginative language and understanding of opposite words.

Early Learning Goal: Communication, Language and Literacy. Children will be able to listen with enjoyment, and respond to stories. They will use language to imagine and recreate roles and experiences.

Resources: Can't You Sleep, Little Bear? by Martin Waddell (Walker); a role-play area set out as a bear cave with dark area covered in blankets, big and small cups and plates, bedding, big chair, rug, toys; different-sized boxes; yellow Cellophane; red/yellow/orange collage materials; black paper; silver foil; a teddy bear.

Organisation: Whole group.

Key vocabulary: Big, little, dark, light, sleep, lantern.

What to do: Read the story to the children. Point out the opposites - big and little, light and dark. Talk about creating a bear cave in the role-play area. Explain that you need to make a dark area by covering the climbing frame or corner with a blanket. Put a small duvet or bed in the dark area for Little Bear and a big comfy chair in the light area.

Make a fire for the light area using collage materials. Help children to make different-sized lanterns by cutting windows out of boxes and adding yellow Cellophane.

Encourage children to take it in turns to role play and retell the story using the dark and light areas and the different-sized lanterns. They could use a teddy bear for Little Bear. To make the 'biggest light of all' try covering the wall outside the cave with dark backing paper and sticking on stars and a giant silver moon made from silver foil.

Activity: Who has the biggest hands?

Learning opportunity: Exploring comparative size and measurement.

Early Learning Goal: Problem Solving, Reasoning and Numeracy. Children will be able to use language such as 'bigger' to describe the size of solid and flat shapes.

Resources: Hands; paper; pencils; paint; rulers.

Organisation: Small group.

Key vocabulary: Measure, bigger, smaller, biggest, smallest, hand spans.

What to do: Help children to draw round their own hands and measure the length with a ruler. Draw round some adult hands. Who has the biggest/smallest hands?

Use paint to make handprints and, starting with the biggest, print them in order of size.

Show children how to stretch their hands into a hand span. Measure this using a ruler. Explain that the children can use their hand spans to measure the lengths of objects in the room.

Ask children to work in pairs to measure different items such as width of table, height of cupboard, length of pencil or book, and of course each other.

Display

Place the construction model vehicles on a road layout and produce name labels on a computer. Display printed hands in strips as a border around the room. Make giant gold frames for the 'big' paintings using pasta and spray paint. Ask children to design frames for the 'small' paintings using tiny dots and patterns.

Week 3
Old and new

Personal, Social and Emotional Development
- At circle time show children a collection of old and new objects. Can they sort them into two groups? How are they different? (PS8)
- Organise a grandparent's day. Invite grandparents or elderly neighbours to visit the nursery. Make special food for the visitors and learn some games to play on the day. (PS5, 7,13)
- Read Nothing by Mick Inkpen (Hodder's Childrens Books). Talk about the different feelings Nothing experiences in the story. (PS3, 4, 5)

Communication, Language and Literacy
- Read Old Bear by Jane Hissey (Red Fox) (see activity opposite). (L4, 7, 13, 17)
- Make invitations for grandparent's day. Ask grandparents to bring in something old and special to show the children such as a photo, book, game or toy. Help children to write their own names. (L17, 18)
- Read *I Want That Room* by Jen Green. Help children to work in pairs to design a new room. (L1, 4, 7)
- Play a cumulative circle game – 'I went to the shops and bought a new _____'. (L7, 8)

Problem Solving, Reasoning and Numeracy
- Talk about how old the children are. How old will they be on their next birthday? Make a chart to show the different birthdays in the group. Which month has the most birthdays? (N1, 2, 6)
- Draw a sheet with ten birthday cakes numbered one to ten. Give the children coloured matchsticks. Can they draw or stick the correct number of candles on each cake? Adapt the rhyme 'Five little candles' from *This Little Puffin*. (N2, 3)
- Sing this song to the tune of 'Hickory dickory dock':
  Is it your birthday today?   (twice)
  How old are you?   (twice)
  You are _____ today. (N1)
- Use a large model clock to introduce o'clock times. (N1, 3)

Knowledge and Understanding of the World
- Look at old photographs of children playing. Talk about the clothes, toys, games and other things that have changed. Encourage children to see differences between past and present. Use a 'then and now' writing frame to help the children to record their ideas. (K8)
- Talk about memories and draw a family tree (see activity opposite). (K8)

Physical Development
- Help the children to pack up the home corner into large cardboard boxes and move to a new house in another area of the room. How can they make the new house different? (PD1, 2, 6)
- Play some old games such as 'Grandmother's Footsteps', 'Farmers in the den' and 'Ring a ring of roses'. (PD2)
- On grandparent's day ask the grandparents to show the children how to play marbles, jacks and tiddly winks. (PD7)

Creative Development
- Design and make a card to send to a new baby. (C2)
- Learn this rhyme and have fun acting it out:
  Comfy shoes, old shoes,
  Hole in the toe shoes.
  Shiny shoes, new shoes,
  Sparkling clean party shoes,
  Which ones will you choose? (C4)
- Draw observational pictures of old and new objects (see PSED) using chalks and pastels on black and white paper. (C3)

Activity: Old Bear

Learning opportunity: Talking, role playing and retelling story using words and pictures.

Early Learning Goal: Communication, Language and Literacy. Children will be able to retell narratives in the correct sequence, drawing on language patterns of stories.

Resources: Old Bear by Jane Hissey (Red Fox); large sack or box; an old teddy bear; wooden bricks; soft toys; paper plant made from plastic flowerpot and green crepe paper; wooden aeroplane; handkerchiefs or squares of material with string tied on each corner; blanket; white paper folded into concertinas; pencils; felt pens.

Organisation: Whole group for story, small groups to use story sack and writing activity.

Key vocabulary: Old, new, vocabulary from book.

What to do: Read the story to the children. Why do they think Old Bear was put in the attic? Talk about all the different ways the toys tried to rescue Old Bear. Act out some of these with the children such as building a tower out of bricks, and making a tower of soft toys. What happened to all these attempts? How did Old Bear get down safely in the end?

Put together a story sack or box with props (see Resources list) so that the children can act out the story in small groups. Use a camcorder to video scenes and watch back with the rest of the group.

Ask children to make their own concertina books of the story by retelling the sequence of events using words and pictures. Help them to scribe a short sentence for each picture. Encourage children to show their stories to the group.

Activity: Family trees

Learning opportunity: Talking and finding out about children's memories and families.

Early Learning Goal: Knowledge and Understanding of the World. Children will be able to find out about past and present events in their own lives, and those of their families and other people they know.

Resources: *Once They Were Giants* by Martin Waddell (MacDonald); paper; pencils; felt pens; photographs or drawings of the children.

Organisation: Whole group for introduction, small groups for recording activity.

Key vocabulary: Old, new, memories, remember, family tree.

What to do: Read *Once There Were Giants* to the children. Talk about memories. Recall any memories that the

grandparents may have shared with the children on grandparent's day. What can the children remember about when they were smaller? Collect these memories, write them on pieces of paper and display them on the wall under the title 'We can remember'.

Help children to think of the names of people in their family, including grandparents, parents and siblings. Be sensitive to children who come from unconventional families. Invite children to draw or stick a photograph of themselves in the middle of a piece of paper. Help them to add the names and draw pictures of their family around the paper to make a simple family tree.

Display

Put old and new items (see PSED) on an interactive display table so children can observe and handle them. Mount and display photos from grandparent's day. Display new baby cards and make photocopies of the best design to sell to parents to raise funds. Paint a big bare brown tree shape and mount and display children's family trees on the branches.

Week 4
Hot and cold

Personal, Social and Emotional Development
- Talk about hot and cold weather. Look at pictures of life in hot and cold countries. Why are the clothes and houses so different? What do children wear in this country when it is hot/cold? (PS1, 6).
- During circle time invite adults to come and talk to the children about visiting or living in hot/cold countries. (PS3, 7)
- Share hot and cold snacks. Try hot soup on a cold day and ice lollies on a hot day. Dip hot chips into cold tomato sauce. (PS2, 8)

Communication, Language and Literacy
- Set up two role-play corners in the room, one for hot weather with beach towels, sunglasses, sun hats, ice creams and buckets and spades, and the other for cold weather, with hats, scarves, gloves and hot buttered toast. (L7, 8)
- Talk about what children like to do when it is hot or cold. Use a writing frame to help record their ideas – 'When it is hot I like to ...' (L8, 17)
- Write a group poem entitled 'What is hot?' Collect lots of 'hot' words to use in the poem such as 'fire', 'sun', 'flames', 'red', and so on. Then write a matching poem using 'cold' words. (L4, 5)
- Make a collection of words that begin with the same initial sounds as hot and cold. Make up funny phrases by putting hot or cold in front of other words such as 'hot hat' and 'cold carrots'. (L9, 10, 12)

Problem Solving, Reasoning and Numeracy
- Make hot and cold drinks for snack time. Use hot water to make hot chocolate and cold water to make orange squash. Draw a chart to show how many children chose each drink. (N1, 2, 6)
- Draw a hat, scarf and gloves and ask children to design a repeating pattern to make matching sets. (N10)

Knowledge and Understanding of the World
- Experiment with ice. Help children to make coloured ice cubes using food colouring. How long does the water take to change into ice? Use vocabulary to describe change – liquid, solid, frozen. Take three trays and fill one with hand-hot water, one with cold and leave one empty. Place an ice cube in each tray. Which ice cube will melt first? (K1, 3, 4)
- Make jelly with the children (see activity opposite). (K1, 3, 4)
- Use a forehead thermometer strip to take children's temperatures. What happens if our temperature is higher than normal? (K2, 3, 4)

Physical Development
- Ask for a volunteer to leave the room while you hide a toy. Help them to find the hiding place by shouting 'hot' when they are near and 'cold' when they are far away. (PD1, 4)
- Try some warm-up exercises to music. What happens to the children's bodies when they are warm? (PD2, 4, 6)
- Use white playdough made with cornflour to make models of animals that live in the snow. Display them on a black sugar paper background. (PD8)

Creative Development
- Talk about 'hot' colours such as red and orange, and 'cold' colours such as blue and green. Ask children to create hot or cold collages using coloured paper, material, paint, and so on. (C2)
- Paint with ice cubes and powder paint. (C3)
- Make weaving frames out of polystyrene trays.

Thread wool across. Provide a selection of red or blue weaving materials such as ribbon, strips of paper, foil and different fabrics. (C2)
- Design clothes for different temperatures (see activity opposite). (C2, 4)

Activity: Making jelly

Learning opportunity: Observing changes in materials using all the senses.

Early Learning Goal: Knowledge and Understanding of the World. Children will be able to investigate objects and materials by using all of their senses as appropriate. They will look closely at similarities, differences and change.

Resources: Jelly; measuring jug; water; fridge; jelly mould; bowls; spoons.

Organisation: Small group.

Key vocabulary: Hot, cold, melt, liquid, set, solid.

What to do: Explain that you are going to make jelly using hot and cold water. Help children to wash their hands carefully. Ask children to tear a block of jelly into cubes. What does the jelly smell of? What does it feel like? Boil a kettle. Point out the steam coming from the kettle as the water boils. Dissolve the jelly in 280ml (half pint) of boiling water. What happens to the jelly as they stir it? Add another 280ml of cold water. Pour the jelly into a mould or an ice cube tray and put it in the fridge.

Talk to the children about what they think will happen to the jelly in the fridge. Check after one hour to see if it has set, or leave overnight. Encourage children to notice how it has changed. Run the mould under warm water and turn onto a plate. Serve jelly with cold ice cream and hot chocolate sauce for a treat!

Activity: What shall I wear...?

Learning opportunity: Working together to design clothes for all weathers.

Early Learning Goal: Creative Development. Children will be able to express and communicate their ideas, thoughts and feelings by using a widening range of materials, suitable tools and a variety of songs.

Resources: Copy of 'What is the weather today?' from *Bobby Shaftoe, Clap your Hands* by Sue Nicholls (A & C Black); two large pieces of card; collage materials; paint.

Organisation: Two small groups.

Key vocabulary: Hot, cold, weather, clothes, temperature.
What to do: Sing 'What is the weather today?' (see Resources). Help children to look outside and think about today's weather. Is it hot or cold outside? Talk about suitable clothes to wear in different sorts of weather (refer to hot/cold role-play areas).

Ask for two volunteers to lie down on a piece of card and be drawn around. Ask one group to design clothes for a hot day and the other for a cold day. Use paint for the faces and bodies and different materials for the clothes. Try to find woollen material for warm jumpers and lycra for swimming trunks, and so on.

Display the two dressed characters in the nursery labelled appropriately – 'Today is hot/cold'.

Display

Make a hot and cold patchwork quilt using contrasting squares or shapes cut from collages, paintings and weaving. Help children to make a table display of a hot or cold country of their choice using books, maps, photographs, paintings, drawings, plastic animals and artefacts.

Week 5
Loud and quiet

Personal, Social and Emotional Development
- Introduce the opposite words, 'loud' and 'quiet'. Ask children to whisper or shout in response to your questions. 'Have you brought your quiet voice?' 'Yes I have, yes I have'. Have they brought any other contrasting voices? (PS2, 7, 8)
- Play 'Chinese whispers'. (PS2, 3, 8)
- Read The Very Noisy Night by Diana Hendry (Little Tiger Press). Talk about how sounds can be scarey at night. What do the children do when they can't sleep? (PS5, 10)

Communication, Language and Literacy
- Make a list of loud and quiet sounds under the headings 'as loud as an elephant' and 'as quiet as a mouse'. (L5. 7. 12)
- Ask children to make up stories about imaginary characters called Loud Luke and Quiet Queenie. Tape-record their stories. (L4, 9, 12)
- Read Peace at Last by Jill Murphy (Walker). Help children to add sound effects using voices, body percussion and/or instruments. Make a picture score of all the sounds the children use. (L1, 4, 17)

Problem Solving, Reasoning and Numeracy
- Write patterns of loud and quiet sounds. Invent suitable symbols for loud and quiet. Ask children to write patterns of eight sounds for others to follow. Choose two instruments or vocal sounds and listen to the patterns. Can the listeners count how many loud or quiet sounds were made? (N1, 2, 10)
- Use instruments and dice to explore musical opposites (see activity opposite). (N1, 2, 3)

Knowledge and Understanding of the World
- Investigate which instrument can make the quietest or loudest sound. Talk about what the instruments are made of. (K1, 3, 4)
- Make shakers using empty cocoa tins (with metal base) filled with sugar or dried beans. Which ones make a quieter sound and why? Try this rhyme:
Shake the sugar, shake the sugar,
Sssh, sssh, sssh, sssh!
Bouncing beans, bouncing beans,
Brrm, brrm, brrm, brrm! (K4, 5)

Physical Development
- Play 'As quiet as a mouse'. Pass a tambourine around the circle without making any sound at all. (PD7)
- Play 'Keeper of the bells'. Choose one child to be blindfolded in the centre of the circle. Ask another child to try a creep up and steal the bells without waking the 'keeper'. (PD2, 4)
- Opposites dance: ask children to move around the room reacting to loud/quiet sounds on a percussion instrument. Try fast/slow and high/low sounds. Organise children into two groups and make the opposite movements at the same time. (PD1, 2, 4)

Creative Development
- Explore conducting (see activity opposite). (C4)
- Make loud and quiet sounds on an instrument. Sit in a circle and ask children to react to the sounds, for instance, put hands on head (loud) and finger on lips (quiet). Ask children to close their eyes and move in response to the sounds. Invite children to play sounds for the group to move to. (C1, 2)

- Enjoy making quiet 'night' and loud 'day' music for the 'Elves and the Shoemaker' from Three Singing Pigs (see Resources). (C2)
- Listen to different examples of loud and quiet recorded music. Ask children to paint loud and quiet pictures as they listen. (C4, 5)

Activity: Dice music

Learning opportunity: Reading numbers and rolling dice to select contrasting sounds.

Early Learning Goal: Problem Solving, Reasoning and Numeracy. Children will be able to say and use number names in order in familiar contexts and recognise numerals one to six.

Resources: Six different musical instruments; one dice with numbers one to six; one dice with words – loud, quiet, fast, slow, long, short; paper; pencils.

Organisation: Small group.

Key vocabulary: Numbers one to six, loud, quiet, fast, slow, long, short.

What to do: Show the children the six different musical instruments and allow time for them to explore the sounds they can make. Label the instruments one to six. Help children to write a sequence of numbers for each other to play.

Introduce the game element by using dice. Children take turns to roll the number dice and play the instrument that matches the number. They can roll the number dice again to find out how many times to make a sound.

Show the children the word dice and talk about musical opposites. Explain to the children that this dice tells them how to play the instrument. Ask them to roll both dice. If the dice say '2' and 'quiet', they must play the instrument labelled '2' quietly and so on.

Activity: Conducting opposites

Learning opportunity: Working together to organise and make musical sounds.

Early Learning Goal: Creative Development. Children will be able to recognise and explore how sounds can be changed, recognise repeated sounds and sound patterns and match movements to music.

Resources: A percussion instrument for each child.

Organisation: Whole group.

Key vocabulary: Start, stop, palms up, fists down, loud, quiet.

What to do: Sit in a circle and give everyone a percussion instrument or sound source. Place them in front of each child and ask them not to touch until they are asked to by the conductor.

Begin by playing the role of the conductor yourself. Stand in the middle of the circle and demonstrate two hand signals to the children – open palms up means start, closed fists down means stop. Ask all children to copy these hand movements. Encourage children to follow the conductor and start and stop playing their instruments. Ask for individuals to conduct the group.

Once they have grasped this, show the children how to adapt the signals to make the music change from loud to quiet. When the conductor's hands are far apart the music should be loud. If the conductor's hands are close together, the musicians should play quietly. Try conducting the whole group, small groups of similar instruments, or soloists.

Display

Paint a huge elephant and a tiny mouse to illustrate the loud and quiet word lists. Ask children to paint or draw pictures of Loud Luke and Quiet Queenie. Compile their stories into a book and display. Make an interactive display of loud and quiet sounds inside identical containers such as variety cereal boxes or opaque plastic bottles using different fillings (beans, rice, sugar, sand, feathers, coins). Ask children to arrange in order of quietest to loudest sounds.

Week 6
Up and down

Personal, Social and Emotional Development
- Talk about the pyjama party and/or opposites parade that will take place this week. What preparations do the children need to make? Discuss refreshments and make invitations. (PS4, 7, 12)
- Play some parachute games (see activity opposite). (PS1, 3, 8)
- Play 'Snakes and ladders'. Talk about the rules of the game. How does it feel to climb up the ladder or slide down the snake? (PS5, 8)

Communication, Language and Literacy
- Make a list of things that go up and down and write them on an open umbrella shape. (L5, 12)
- Give four or five children a card each showing a different character (picture and word). Make up a story using the characters. Ask children to stand up every time their character is mentioned and then sit down again. Try adding actions for each of the characters. Invite children to make up a story for the group to listen to. (L3, 4, 7)
- Sing the nursery rhyme 'Hickory dickory dock'. Ask children to draw a sequence of pictures to retell the rhyme and label them with the words 'up' and 'down'. (L4, 13, 17, 19)

Problem Solving, Reasoning and Numeracy
- Make a collection of other positional opposites such as in/out, in front/behind, above/below, upstairs/downstairs and so on. Ask children to hide a small toy or counter and then describe where it is. (N12)
- Sing 'The rides at the fair go up and down' to the tune of 'The wheels on the bus'. Add actions and extra verses: 'One boy at the fair…', 'Two girls at the fair…', 'Three teddies…', 'Four cats..' and 'Five pigs…'. (N1, 2)

Knowledge and Understanding of the World
- Explore floating and sinking. Make a collection of items that will either float (stay up) or sink (go down) in water. Ask children to work in pairs. Can they find two things that float and two things that sink? (K1, 4)

- Make boats from off-cuts of soft wood, straws, nails, card and bottle tops. Do they all float? (K5, 6)
- Have fun building tall towers using bricks. (K4, 5)

Physical Development
- Play 'Changes' (see activity opposite). (PD2, 3, 4)
- Borrow a small trampoline. Encourage children to take turns jumping up and down. Who can keep going the longest? Take care to follow safety precautions. (PD2, 7)
- Pretend to be 'Jack in the boxes'. (PD1, 2)

Creative Development
- Sing 'The Grand Old Duke of York', 'Goosey, Goosey Gander' and 'Jack and Jill'. Help children to act out the rhymes. (C4, 5)
- Cover the top and underside of a table with sugar paper. Ask children to paint decorations on the top and bottom of the table. Which is easier to do? Talk about famous artists who painted 'upside down' such as Leonardo da Vinci. (C3, 5)
- Ask children to draw a simple up and down pattern onto a small polystyrene tile. Use rollers to cover the tile with printing ink. Press the tile face down on the paper. Make two or three prints before adding more paint. (C2, 3)

Activity: Parachute games

Learning opportunity: Playing a circle game with the parachute.

Early Learning Goal: Personal, Social and Emotional Development. Children will continue to be interested, excited and motivated to learn. They will work as part of a group, taking turns and sharing fairly.

Resources: Small parachute or sari cut in half and sewn into a square; small balls; small teddies.

Organisation: Whole group.

Key vocabulary: Up, down, side, edge, balls, bounce, float.

What to do: Sit in a circle and ask children to hold onto a handle or the edge of the parachute or sari. Gently make the parachute move up and down and chant 'up and down' as it moves. Try shaking the parachute and chant 'side to side'.

Place some small balls on the parachute and make them bounce up and down. Try singing:

The balls are bouncing up and down,
Up and down, up and down.
The balls are bouncing up and down,
As we sing.
(Tune: 'The wheels on the bus')

Ask children to stand up and hold the edges of the parachute high up in the air. Can they make a ball fall through the hole in the centre of the cloth? Try bouncing teddies on the parachute and sing 'The teddies are jumping up and down' as before.

Activity: Changes

Learning opportunity: Changing level, speed and direction using large and small equipment.

Early Learning Goal: Physical Development. Children will be able to move with control and coordination. They will travel around, under, over and through balancing and climbing equipment.

Resources: Large space; selection of large and small equipment such as climbing frame, slide, tunnels, balance beams, hoops, beanbags and so on.

Organisation: Whole group.

Key vocabulary: Up, down, fast, slow, over, under, forwards, backwards.

What to do: Explain to the children that they are going to play a game called 'Changes'. Ask children to stand in a circle and move around the room in a circle. When they hear one tap on the tambourine they have to change direction. Practise this until children can respond quickly. Introduce another change – two taps means change speed (fast/slow), three taps means change level (high up/low down).

Set up a circuit of large and small equipment for the children to go round. Make sure there are lots of opportunities to go up and down slides, through tunnels, up climbing frames, jump up and down, climb in and out of hoops, and so on. Try playing 'Changes' as they go round. Be sure to emphasise safety.

Ask children to count how many circuits they can complete in five minutes. Use a stopwatch to time circuits. Who can complete the circuit in the fastest time? Give out certificates to everyone who tries hard. Provide refreshments. You could use this as a sponsored fundraising event as part of the final week.

Display

Make a display of things that go up and down such as umbrellas, rockets, aeroplanes, birds, balloons, slides, and so on. Create a boat show in the water tray to display the children's model boats. Mount and display the children's press print pictures around the room.

Bringing It All Together

Pyjama party
Talk to the children about the pyjama party. This could be a special session culminating in an opposites parade during the last half hour to which parents, carers and friends can be invited. At the start of the topic, inform parents of the date of the special event and any help or resources you may need.

Preparation
Explain to the children that the pyjama party will be a fun way to explore the opposites 'night' and 'day' and so enjoy doing 'night time' things during the day at nursery. Ask children to come to nursery wearing pyjamas, dressing gowns and slippers. The opposites parade at the end will be an opportunity to show things that they have made during the topic and explain what they have learned to their families and friends.

Activities
Set up a variety of activities based on going to bed and night-time. Put teddy bears and dolls to bed in the home corner. Read bedtime stories and books about nocturnal animals. Talk about bath time, cleaning teeth and other bedtime routines. Sing bedtime songs and lullabies. At snack time, sit in a circle on duvets, and share midnight snacks of hot chocolate and cookies. Ice happy and sad face biscuits to give out to the visitors at the parade. Make fruit kebabs with alternate pieces of different fruit. Make fruit cocktails using cold tea, lemonade, fruit juice, chopped fruit and ice. Serve with long and short straws in big and small cups.

Ask children to bring in torches labelled with their name. In a dark room, enjoy torch dancing to music. Help children to follow the beams of light from their torches as they dance around the room. Remember to have a stock of spare torches and batteries to avoid disappointments. If an overhead projector is available, make shadows and enjoy a shadow puppet show.

Opposites parade
Help children in pairs to dress up or find objects to illustrate different opposites such as big/small, short/tall, fast/slow, high/low, hot/cold, new/old, happy/sad, good/bad, heavy/light, black/white, dirty/clean, and so on.

Show displays of children's work during the topic and teach songs and rhymes from previous weeks. Join in the opposites dance from week five (Physical Development). Play an opposite hunting game: collect pictures showing lots of opposite pairs. Cut up an old book or magazines. Hide one of each pair around the room, or outside. Give the remaining cards to groups of children and an adult. Can they find the missing pair?

Resources

All books were available from leading booksellers at the time of writing

Resources to collect
- Hand mirrors.
- Opposite books, puzzles and games.
- Camera.
- Big and small teddy bears and clothes.
- Magnifying glasses.
- Old photographs of children.
- Pictures of hot/cold climates.
- Forehead thermometer.
- Ice cube trays.
- Parachute.
- Trampoline.

Everyday resources
- Bottle lids, corks, tubes, wooden spoons, paper plates, polystyrene trays and large and small boxes for modelling.
- Papers and cards of different weights, colours and textures, for example sugar paper, corrugated card, sticky paper, silver and shiny papers.
- Dry powder paints for mixing, and mixed paints for covering large areas and printing.
- Different-sized paintbrushes from household brushes and rollers to thin brushes for delicate work, and a variety of paint mixing containers.
- A variety of drawing and colouring pencils, crayons, chalks, pastels and felt pens.
- Salt dough ingredients and cutters.
- Softwood, hammers, nails, lolly sticks, and bottle lids for woodwork.
- Tape recorder.
- Percussion instruments.

Stories
- *Charlie and Lola's Opposites* by Lauren Child (Orchard).
- *Elephant Elephant: A Book of Opposites* by Francesco Pittau (HNA Books)
- *Dogger* by Shirley Hughes (Red Fox).
- *Where's my Teddy?* by Jez Alborough (Walker).
- *Can't You Sleep, Little Bear?* by Martin Waddell (Walker).
- *Nothing* by Mick Inkpen (Hodder Children's Books).
- *Old Bear* by Jane Hissey (Red Fox).
- *I Want That Room: Moving House* by Jen Green (1 Wayland).
- *Once There Were Giants* by Martin Waddell (Walker).
- *The Very Noisy Night* by Diana Hendry (Little Tiger Press).
- *Peace at Last* by Jill Murphy (Walker).
- *Brave Charlotte* by Anu Stohner (Bloomsbury).
- *You and Me, Little Bear* by Martin Waddell (Walker).
- *Happy Dog, Sad Dog* by Sam Lloyd (Walker).
- *Go Wild With Opposites!* by Neal Layton (Chrysalis).

Non-fiction
- *My First Book of Opposites* by Kim Deegan (Bloomsbury).
- *My First Book of Opposites* by Peter Patilla (OUP).
- *Elmer's Opposites* by David McKee (Andersen Press).
- *Big and Small: An Animal Opposites Book* by Lisa Bullard (Capstone Press).
- *Maisy Big, Maisy Small* by Lucy Cousins (Walker).

Songs and rhymes
- *Bobby Shaftoe, Clap Your Hands* by Sue Nicholls (A & C Black).
- *Three Tapping Teddies* by Kaye Umansky (A & C Black).
- *This Little Puffin* by Elizabeth Matterson (Puffin).
- *High Low Dolly Pepper: Developing Music Skills with Young Children* by Veronica Clark (A & C Black).
- *Three Singing Pigs* by Kaye Umansky (A & C Black).
- *Bingo Lingo* by Helen MacGregor (A & C Black).

Collecting Evidence of Children's Learning

Monitoring children's development is an important task. Keeping a record of children's achievements, interests and learning styles will help you to see progress and will draw attention to those who are having difficulties for some reason. If a child needs additional professional help, such as speech therapy, your records will provide valuable evidence.

Records should be the result of collaboration between group leaders, parents and carers. Parents should be made aware of your record keeping policies when their child joins your group. Show them the type of records you are keeping and make sure they understand that they have an opportunity to contribute. As a general rule, your records should form an open document. Any parent should have access to records relating to his or her child. Take regular opportunities to talk to parents about children's progress. If you have formal discussions regarding children about whom you have particular concerns, a dated record of the main points should be kept.

Keeping it manageable

Records should be helpful in informing group leaders, adult helpers and parents and always be for the benefit of the child. The golden rule is to make them simple, manageable and useful.

Observations will basically fall into three categories:
- **Spontaneous records:** Sometimes you will want to make a note of observations as they happen, for example, a child is heard counting cars accurately during a play activity, or is seen to play collaboratively for the first time.

- **Planned observations:** Sometimes you will plan to make observations of children's developing skills in their everyday activities. Using the learning opportunity identified for an activity will help you to make appropriate judgements about children's capabilities and to record them systematically.

To collect information:
- talk to children about their activities and listen to their responses;
- listen to children talking to each other;
- observe children's work such as early writing, drawings, paintings and 3D models. (Keeping photocopies or photographs is useful.)

Sometimes you may wish to set up 'one off' activities for the purposes of monitoring development. Some pre-school groups, for example, ask children to make a drawing of themselves at the beginning of each term to record their progressing skills in both co-ordination and observation. Do not attempt to make records after every activity!

- **Reflective observations:** It is useful to spend regular time reflecting on the children's progress. Aim to make some brief comments about each child every week.

Informing your planning

Collecting evidence about children's progress is time consuming and it is important that it is useful. When you are planning, use the information you have collected to help you to decide what learning opportunities you need to provide next for children. For example, a child who has poor pencil or brush control will benefit from more play with dough or construction toys to build the strength of hand muscles.

Example of recording chart

Name: Miriam Lewis		D.O.B. 01.04.04		Date of entry: 12.12.08	
Term	Personal, Social and Emotional Development	Communication, Language and Literacy	Problem Solving, Reasoning and Numeracy	Knowledge and Understanding of the World	Physical Development	Creative Development
ONE	Confident to try new activities. Friendly to adults and other children. 2.10.08 MM	Enjoys listening to stories, especially *Where's My Teddy?* Can recognise own name. 28.10.08 RA	Recognises numbers 1-10. Enjoyed pattern work. Knew date of birthday. 12.12.08 MM	Enjoyed work on family tree. Knew family names and relationships. Asks lots of questions. 6.11.08 PB	Lacks confidence on large apparatus. Good control of tools. 21.11.08 RA	Joins in singing and enjoys all drama activities. Enjoys painting. 3.12.08 PB
TWO						
THREE						

Skills overview of six-week plan

Week	Topic Focus	Personal, Social and Emotional Development	Communication, Language and Literacy	Problem Solving, Reasoning and Numeracy	Knowledge and Understanding of the World	Physical Development	Creative Development
1	Happy and sad	Talking; Taking turns; Discussing feelings	Making up stories; Exploring words; Enjoying books	Shapes; Number rhymes	Using technology; Designing and making puppets	Throwing and catching; Handling tools; Dancing	Singing; Painting; Making masks; Drama
2	Big and small	Listening; Care of others; Awarness of safety	Role-play; Extending vocabulary; Initial sounds; Writing names	Creating patterns; Measuring; Weighing	Observing; Constructing	Moving with control and imagination	Painting; Singing; Making sounds; Drama
3	Old and new	Awarness of needs; Planning as a group; Discussing feelings	Retelling story; Writing for a purpose; Taking turns	Using numbers; Counting; Number rhymes; Measuring time	Observing; Talking and writing about past	Moving with control and coordination; Using malleable materials; Using a range of equipment	Using materials; Singing; Drama; Drawing
4	Hot and cold	Awarness of needs; Listening; Sharing snacks	Role-play; Writing poetry; Recognising initial sounds	Using numbers; Counting; Creating patterns	Investigating; Observing change; Asking questions	Moving safely; Moving with control and coordination; Using a range of equipment	Collage; Weaving; Using materials
5	Loud and quiet	Taking turns; Listening; Discussing feelings	Extending vocabulary; Making up stories; Listening to stories; Exploring sounds	Creating patterns; Recognising numbers; Counting	Investigating; Constructing; Asking questions	Moving with control and coordination; Recognising body changes; Using malleable materials	Making sounds' Using instruments; Listening; Painting
6	Up and down	Collaborative planning; Taking turns; Sharing	Exploring words; Making up stories; Writing for a purpose	Using mathematical language; Number rhymes; Counting	Investigating; Constructing	Awareness of space; Moving with control and coordination; Using a range of equipment	Singing; Drama, Painting; Printing

Home links

The theme of 'Opposites' lends itself to useful links with children's homes and families. Through working together children and adults gain respect for each other and build comfortable and confident relationships.

Establishing partnerships
- Keep parents informed about the topic of 'Opposites' and the themes for each week. By understanding the work of the group, parents will enjoy the involvement of contributing ideas, time and resources.
- Photocopy the parent's page for each child to take home.
- Ask parents for help in inviting grandparents or elderly relatives or neighbours to your grandparent's day.
- Invite families, carers and friends to come to the special opposites parade at the end of the topic.
- Invite parents to take photographs at the grandparent's day and the opposites parade.

Visiting enthusiasts
- Invite adults who have lived in or visited hot/cold countries to visit the nursery and talk about their experiences. Make sure that visitors are well briefed so that children's attention can be sustained.

Resource requests
- Invite parents to bring in old items for a hands-on display of machines, books, toys and photographs.
- Ask parents to help children find out about family members and their interesting life stories.
- Ask parents to bring in a photograph of their child to put on the family tree.

Pyjama party
- Ask parents to encourage children to come to nursery in their pyjamas for the party.
- At the event, it may be helpful to have additional adults to help the children prepare and serve the refreshments, play games and take part in the opposites parade.